D0811026

Floppy's Fun Phonics

Written by Kate Ruttle and Annemarie Young
Illustrated by Nick Schon, based on the original characters
created by Roderick Hunt and Alex Brychta

OXFORD
UNIVERSITY PRESS

Read the sentence on this card. Which picture matches the card?

Dad is sad.

Read the captions on these cards. Which card matches the picture?

rats on a sack

cats on a sock

6

Read the captions on these cards. Which card matches the picture?

a hen and a bug

a hat on a dog

Read the sentences on these cards. Which card matches the picture?

Run in the sun.

Sit in the sun.

Read the sentences on these cards. Which card matches the picture?

A dog can sit.

A dog can run.

Read the sentences on these cards. Can you match each card to its picture?

A dog is a pet.

The dog is wet.

Read the sentences on these cards. Can you match each card to its picture?

Run and hop.

Run to the top.

Read the sentences on these cards. Can you match each card to its picture?

Biff is on a mug.

It is a big red bug.

18

Read the sentences on these cards. Can you match each card to its picture?

Biff is in a sack.

A doll is in a backpack.

21

Spot the difference

Find the five differences in the two pictures of Floppy.